The Curse
of
Conservatism

By

Coleman Luck

The Sandstar Group

The Sandstar Group
POB 3613
Oakhurst, CA 93644
818-773-1924
www.colemanluck.com

ISBN-10: 0-9888888-3-1
ISBN-13: 978-0-9888888-3-8

Cover design by Carel Gage Luck

2000 years ago Jesus Christ said that
His Kingdom was not of this world.
His followers have been trying to prove
Him wrong ever since.

This book is dedicated with love to my oldest son,
Coleman Luck III, for his tireless support,
wisdom and encouragement.

Contents:

Preface

A New Forrest Gump

There is a Forrest Gump aspect to my life. Do you remember that classic 1994 film? While being goodhearted, but rather ignorant, Forrest finds himself present at very unique historical events. That has been true for me as well. Let me give you a list:

1963 – in Dallas for the Kennedy assassination. (No, I was not in the book depository building. I was several miles away. And the whole thing wrecked my birthday party.)

1968 – in Vietnam just outside Saigon for the massive Tet Offensive. (I was awakened by the huge army ammo dump at Long Binh exploding into the sky. It was the beginning of an interesting day.)

1972 – in Washington for the Watergate Scandal. (I worked just a few blocks from the White House.)

1974 – in southern California for... what?

Well, as they say, therein lies a story.

When I was in my late 20's I had no inkling that I would wind up in Hollywood as a television writer and producer. I was working in communications, advertising and marketing within the evangelical Christian world.

During that period of my life, I spent several years as Supervisor of Production and Talent for WMBI and the Moody Radio Network, a ministry of the Moody Bible Institute in Chicago. From there I went to Christianity Today magazine in Washington, DC where, among other things, I was Advertising Manager.

From the time I left Moody, everything became increasingly strange. I reached one pinnacle of that strangeness in 1974.

At the start of that year I was recruited to join the leadership staff of an odd little organization in Buena Park, California called the Christian Freedom Foundation. Its offices were in a small shabby building across from Knott's Berry Farm. The organization had existed for several decades as a platform for conservative economic philosophy, but the founder was very old and had retired.

The young president who had taken over was a man named H. Edward Rowe. Mr. Rowe wanted to bring about significant change in the organization and recruited me and others to help him establish and achieve new goals. I became marketing director. I was 28 years old. Several other young men were brought on board to head other divisions.

From the start, my interest was in dealing with critical social issues from a Christian perspective. I wanted Christians to understand and confront the massive changes taking place all around us and I wanted us to do it issue by issue as citizens of the Kingdom of God basing our perspectives and actions on the Bible.

Because Mr. Rowe promised a platform for such thought leadership, I moved my family across the United States from Virginia to participate in what I believed would be a new organization speaking with creativity and Christian concern in an increasingly chaotic world. A friend of mine from Christianity Today moved his family the same distance to join the staff. All of us believed in what we were doing.

I'd been there for only a few months when something strange began to happen. Mr. Rowe started going away for long meetings in other states. None of our leadership team went with him and when he returned he shared nothing about what had transpired. Years later I discovered the truth.

Mr. Rowe and a number of evangelical and conservative political leaders were meeting to map out the creation of an evangelical Christian political movement. Their intention was to marry Christian thought with right-wing political activism. At these meetings were men like Bill Bright, president of Campus Crusade for Christ and Arizona Congressman John Conlan.

Before Christmas 1974 arrived, powerful men with money made an offer to Mr. Rowe to fund and change his organization. He accepted that offer and the Christian Freedom Foundation became the corporate structure for what later was called the Moral Majority.

Mr. Rowe didn't tell any of us about what had happened. Just before Christmas he simply fired every one of the new senior staff that he had hired only months before. My young family and I, as well as other young men and their families, were cut off with no apologies, explanations or termination packages.

Needless to say, it was a difficult time. Several of us were a continent away from our home areas and had to find ways to move back on our own. Only years later did I learn about the conspiracy to politicize evangelicals that had caused it all. However, looking back, there were shadows of it that were visible from the start.

Mr. Rowe knew what he was doing in getting rid of me. During the few months that I was on his staff, we had many discussions about the responsibilities of Christians in American society. While at that time I considered myself a conservative, even as a young man I didn't believe the Christian faith should be co-opted by any political agenda and I said so. I wanted to see Christians deeply involved in their world, taking the love and message of Jesus to the heartbroken and lost. And I didn't want that message to be clouded.

I believed then and I believe now, that citizenship in the Kingdom of Heaven is the first priority. Far beyond any worldly affiliation, a disciple of Jesus owes his allegiance to that Kingdom and its King. To be a citizen of that Kingdom means doing your part to carry out the Great Commission that Jesus gave. It means being "in the world, but not of it." This does not preclude passionate involvement in society. In fact, it demands it. But it defines that involvement with unique parameters.

I thought the discussions with Mr. Rowe were enjoyable and productive. I liked him and he seemed to agree with me about the Christian's role in society. Being young, I wasn't sophisticated enough to understand the truth.

We had started a magazine. The first issue came out that fall. In the second issue Mr. Rowe wanted me to hype conservative Arizona Congressman John Conlan. This did not sit well. I couldn't understand why he wanted it done. Conlan struck me as a puffed up cartoon character. I didn't see the point of adding more gas to his balloon. Were we in the business of promoting politicians? Not in my view.

A talented young artist was on my staff. I assigned her the task of drawing Conlan's portrait. When it was finished I told her to put tiny gold stars in his eyes. Mr. Rowe did not see the humor in that fine piece of art.

So there I was, a Forrest Gump-like character, standing ignorantly and ineffectually against a mighty crud-filled tsunami that was about to sweep out from that laughable little organization and inundate the entire United States.

It was an educational moment in my life – one of many. Over the years I've thought about the men involved. Were they bad men? No, at least most weren't. Some, such as Bill Bright, had done great things for the Kingdom of God. But without knowing it, they had lost their way. The desire for power – of course, all for the best purposes – had worked its subtle corruption.

H. Edward Rowe was not a bad man. In my opinion, he was a bright man who was ethically weak with stars in his eyes. For such men the end justifies the means. He and all the others were suffering from cancerous messianic complexes. They were not the first evangelicals to fall to such error, nor will they be the last.

What happened to the young staff at the Christian Freedom Foundation was a tiny foretaste of the cold, calculating, mercenary, unbiblical and unchristian nature of the forces that were about to warp the heart of the evangelical movement in America.

There in Buena Park, at the very foundation of what became the Moral Majority, it was established that people did not matter. They were expendable. The great end of creating a Christian society justified any means.

Little wonder that such a movement has failed so miserably.

It has been almost 40 years since those awful days in the Christian Freedom Foundation. How odd the name rings now in my memory. It wasn't about Christian "freedom" at all. It was about Machiavellian manipulation to gain political power. Four decades later, the evangelical Christian Church in America has reaped what those men sowed.

Chapter One

How in the World Did
We Get Here?

The first eleven slaves arrived in Virginia from Africa in 1619. The first of my Luck ancestors arrived in Virginia from England in 1633. I don't know the names of any of the African slaves, but my ancestor's name was Robert Luck. He had sailed to the British colony on H.M.S. Bonaventure and when he landed he was 24 years old.

Robert was a courageous young man seeking his fortune and Virginia was a dangerous place in 1633. I'm proud of my ancestor's courage. I like to think that, had I been young during those years, I might have sailed with him.

Robert Luck and his descendents did well for themselves in Virginia. They seem to have been respected members of their communities. Most were Christians, members of the Episcopal Church and the Presbyterian Church, with a scattering of Baptists and Quakers around the edges. The Luck ancestors did well in Virginia because they were able to acquire significant amounts of land. And to work that land they bought slaves.

Slaves were a serious investment. The market value of a strong, young male field hand was about that of a Mercedes Benz today. Obviously you had to be careful about what you were buying. After all, in theory, it was a lifetime investment with no manufacturer's warranty in case your "equipment" broke down.

Just like used cars, the price for slaves was variable based upon a number of factors. Children were cheap, in today's money maybe only a couple of hundred dollars each. With a child you had a long wait before the equipment began to function at optimal performance levels and children often died young. On the other end of the age spectrum, you'd pay a couple of thousand dollars for a slave who was an excellent seamstress or cook, but who was getting rather close to the graveyard.

Just as we must take care of our cars if we want them to continue running, slave owners had to care for their slaves. It was only reasonable. You wanted to get as many "miles" out of them as you could.

One of my ancestors owned a tobacco factory. To operate it, he employed 100 slaves. I would imagine that working in a building was better than chopping tobacco in a field under the hot sun. Slaves in his factory got two new changes of clothes each winter – hand-sewn by my ancestor's wife and daughters. That's a lot of sewing. It sounds like my ancestor took pretty good care of his equipment.

Does this horrify you? It should. And, for very personal reasons it horrifies me. I would love to believe that, had I lived in that day, the clarity of my moral vision would have shown me the hellish inhumanity of slavery. I would love to believe that my moral courage would have given me the strength to do everything that I possibly could to end it.

Unfortunately, most of us do not rise above the evils of our time. Had I lived in that day, very likely I would have been deeply "troubled" by the "necessity" of slavery. However, due to that "necessity," I would have owned slaves. It would have been a matter of economic survival. Without them, how would I feed my family? Without them, how could I run the ancestral agri-business? After all, there were few machines to take their place and I was supplying the needs of a society for clothing and good smokes. Probably, I would argue that it wasn't my fault I was born on a plantation. It was God's will and I had to make the best of it.

Yes, and I'm sure that I would have made the best of it. I'd like to believe that, because I was a Christian, I would have been a "humane" slave owner, just and kind to my slaves as every Christian slave owner should be.

By definition, a truly Christian slave owner did "right" by his servants (a much nicer word than slaves), which meant that he didn't abuse them. He gave them adequate food and shelter. He didn't separate families. And of course, he maintained them when they got old and weren't able to work anymore.

That was the ideal. Is that the way all Christian slave owners acted? If you think so you're a lot less cynical than I am. Power corrupts and when you have almost absolute power over the life of another human being, no matter who you are, there's a good chance you will be corrupted.

Thank God, I wasn't born in those days. Slave ownership was a curse, not only on our nation, but especially on my family. My great-grandfather and other ancestors lost everything after the Civil War. And I say this with deep sorrow, the descendents of Robert Luck deserved to lose everything for having built their wealth on such a terrifying evil.

What's the point of all this? Well, here is an interesting fact: My southern ancestors were good solid conservative Christians. Utilizing the best conservative values of their culture they were dead wrong in the middle of the greatest moral crisis of their time.

Why? Because over the centuries, their conservative values such as honesty, hard work, patriotism, love of freedom, respect for tradition, loyalty to family, belief in capitalism, commitment to honor, etc., were not enough. Their conservative values failed them because, in themselves, such values are malleable, easily warped by the selfishness, corruption and fears of any generation.

Such values will always warp if they are not measured against an absolutely true and timeless standard. The only such standard is a Christian faith based upon the Bible as the inspired, inerrant Word of God. All others have proven to be insufficient because they attempt to transform actions while leaving the depths of the inner person unchanged.

My ancestors were church-going Christians. So, if Christianity is a true and timeless standard, how could they have failed? Quite simply, because they let the conservative values of their time, molded by what they considered economic necessity, define their Christian faith instead of the other way around. To have stood against those conservative values would have been too costly.

What is the central truth of historic Christianity? Jesus Christ, the Son of God, came from Heaven to pay the price for our sins as our Substitute – to buy us all from the slave market of spiritual depravity. We were owned by Satan and Jesus paid the price for our freedom with His blood.

If I have accepted His gift of salvation, if I have allowed Him to break the chains that bound my soul, if I know that before God all men and women are equal, shouldn't I as a Christian strive for freedom and equality for all people whenever possible?

How can I own a person when, according to Jesus, that person is my neighbor and my brother or sister? How can I own a person when that person's deepest welfare should be my primary concern? This timeless standard of Biblical truth was subtly twisted by a conservative cultural agenda.

The argument went something like this: Because Africans are intellectually and morally inferior it is the white person's responsibility before God to care for them. The best way for this to be accomplished was for them to remain in servitude. Why are they an inferior race? Because of what happened in Genesis chapter 9. Noah cursed their ancient ancestor Canaan, thereby placing all of them in perpetual servitude for all of time. As far as the issue of slavery is concerned, does the Bible speak against it? It does not. In fact, it urges slaves to be obedient to their masters.

It's interesting to note that the Christian abolitionists of their day were considered "radicals" and "liberals." Truthfully, most people in both the north and the south hated them because they insisted on thinking and acting "Christianly" no matter the cost.

You and I live in a more "enlightened" age. Slavery is no longer the burning issue and a new "conservatism" has arisen that has beckoned to Christians. From the 1970's onward it has instructed us in how we are to function within our culture. For decades, we have accepted that instruction as authoritative. In the process, we have allowed our faith to be syncretized with a political agenda. We made the Republican Party our agent for cultural and societal transformation.

Was that a good idea? Should we have allowed the conservative Republican agenda to marry evangelical thought? Has the GOP been a good bedfellow? How did this "romance" that led us into a Republican bed ever begin?

Chapter Two

Welcome to Bed

Decades ago most evangelical Christians agreed with "social" conservatives that our country was in a "crisis." We agreed that there was a desperate need for political, legislative and judicial transformation. Based upon that common ground, conservative Republicans invited us to come in and share the bed called "Traditional Values."

And it seemed both logical and practical that we should do so. Though they may not have been "Christians" in the sense that Jesus Christ was their Savior and Lord, these people revered our "moral philosophy" and "cultural traditions." They were the first to agree with us that our country was founded on Christian "principles." Wasn't it only practical that we join with them to re-shape this country into what it ought to be?

For almost forty years many evangelical leaders have done just that, with millions of the faithful staunch-ly behind them. They have made common cause with powerful individuals and groups. They have worked to establish coalitions. They have strategized. Endless hours have been spent raising funds and campaigning. Evan-gelical leaders became power-brokers fawned over by the wealthy conservative elite. As the decades passed, they delivered at the polls, which culminated in a great victory, the election of George W. Bush and a Republi-can majority in both the House and the Senate.

Not only were evangelical leaders inside the polit-ical tent, they paid for the tent. Not only did they de-mand a seat at the table, they cooked the food, served it and ate it. And after a romantic dinner, that large soft Republican bed offered a lot of pleasure. The Grand Old Party was almost the evangelical Christian party. The syncretism was virtually complete. Was that good? Many said yes.

A true story: Early in the new century, a Chris-tian young person of my close acquaintance was working in Washington, D.C. as a staff member for a Republican committee of the U. S. Senate. Constantly, he faced well-educated people who thought they were Christians because they were Republicans.

At one social event someone asked him if he were a Christian. Just to see their response he replied with all seriousness, "I'm a Republican." They didn't bat an eye. For them, that was quite acceptable. No other statement of faith was needed.

Does this horrify you? If you are a Christian, it should. By making common cause under the tent of "traditional values," we have given primacy to those values and allowed them to define what it means, both to be a Christian and to act "Christianly" in our society.

Just as my slave-owning ancestors in the Old South shaped their faith and practice to match the "conservative agenda" of their culture, so we have reshaped our faith and practice to match the conservative agenda that was presented to us. We became warriors for a Christian America.

Dream with me for a minute: Wouldn't it be wonderful if we could guarantee that every judge, legislator, governor and President was an evangelical Christian and a good conservative Republican? Don't you agree with me that if that happened, in less than a generation we could solve most of the problems of our nation and reshape it into what it was, taking back what we lost due to the narcissistic sloppiness and moral turpitude of Liberals and Progressives?

If we got rid of Liberals and Progressives from every level of government wouldn't we be on the way to a truly moral and Christian society? Oh, of course, it wouldn't be perfect, but just imagine wiping out abortion, taking care of the illegal alien problem, getting prayer back into our public schools, cleaning up the stinking mess in Hollywood and the porn industry. Just imagine wiping out all those gun control freaks who want to destroy the Second Amendment.

If you are a Christian and after reading those words, you sent up a resounding "AMEN," I have bad news for you. You have succumbed to the First Temptation hidden in the Curse of Conservatism. You have allowed a political agenda to define the meaning of societal transformation and the methods for achieving it. You have come to believe that the moral transformation of a culture can be imposed successfully from the top down. It is clear from history that this is not so.

The society of ancient Rome was decadent almost beyond description. It reeked of pedophilia. Male and female prostitution was rampant. Unwanted babies were left in open fields to die. Brutality and bloody violence were the order of the day. In one series of "games" 10,000 people were murdered for the pleasure of a screaming drunken crowd. Most governmental leaders were vile.

Into that evil culture the Church of Jesus Christ was planted without the slightest power or prestige. For over two hundred years Christians suffered within that empire, hounded and, in some cases, murdered for their beliefs. The only power they had was the power of a risen Savior who had transformed their lives. That power transformed the Roman world one person at a time.

However, at a certain moment in history everything changed. Christians gained political power. They took control of the government. Initially, much good was done. Some of the most flagrant abuses and horrors were ended. But in the process of wielding power, the Church became utterly corrupted. As it syncretized, much of its moral authority was lost and we have suffered the consequences ever since.

The problem is this: When Christian moral standards are imposed on a society by political and/or military conquest an inevitable process begins. First, there is a period of relief and apparent success for the agenda of the victors. The most egregious wrongs are righted. For a while the vanquished (those who disagree with the new moral order) are intimidated into silence. But very soon they begin to regain power as the society, never having experienced real spiritual transformation, grows tired of restraint.

Then one of two things happens. Either the "victors" and their laws are swept away leaving that society even more decadent than before, or the "victors" tighten control and enforce their laws through increasing oppression. Every time the Christian Church has become enmeshed with political and/or military power her true mission has been compromised no matter which direction society has turned.

In His greatest hour of crisis Jesus proclaimed that His Kingdom was not of this world. Christians have been trying to prove Him wrong ever since. American Conservatism is a curse because, in our desperation for societal change, it tempted us to believe that if we didn't force collective transformation through political action there was no hope. The nation was lost. This temptation to trust in worldly power is precisely what Jesus refused all of His life, especially during His temptation in the wilderness.

What was at the heart of those three "temptings" by Satan? The Prince of Darkness tried to make Him agree that the "ends" could justify the "means," that a false alliance and a grab for easy power were permissible in order to accomplish the transformation of human society.

Jesus was tempted to make common cause with the Power behind the thrones of this world in order to establish His Kingdom in a different way and time than God had intended. Sad to say, many times throughout history, His Church has fallen to the temptation that He resisted. Over the past 40 years American evangelicals have been sucked into that deep pit.

In my direct lineage I have a strange little great-great (several more greats) grandmother. I love her story. What guts she had. There's a statue of her at the state house in Boston. Her name was Mary Barrett Dyer. She was a friend and associate of Roger Williams (also one of my direct ancestors and the true founder of religious freedom in this country). Mary Barrett Dyer was hung by the Puritans on June 1, 1660. I'm proud to be one of her grandsons.

Do you want to know why Mary was hung? She wouldn't stop teaching the Bible. Did they string her up because she was teaching heresy? No. She *was* a heresy. They hung her because women weren't supposed to teach the Bible and she just wouldn't stop. That was her gift and she felt called to use it. She felt called to confront the injustice of her society and that society was devoutly "Christian."

Mary must have been a good teacher otherwise no one would have noticed. Three hundred years after her death the court that hung her ordered a statue erected in her honor. On it they placed a quote from some of her writings. "My life not availeth me in comparison to the liberty of truth." It's been my observation that far too often Christians who speak the truth to other Christians get hung.

If you think establishing morality in the United States and healing our diseased nation is going to happen through the Christian church collectively exerting political power may I suggest that we take a brief journey through time? Let's start under the tree where my great-great grandmother is slowly turning in the breeze.

From there we could go to the Salem Witch Trials in New England that took place in part under a fine Christian pastor named Cotton Mather. And I'm not being sarcastic when I say that. He really was a fine Christian man. Did his actions and the actions of others in trying to purify their society accomplish their goals? The result was the exact opposite. Their actions weakened the Christian faith in their day and afterward.

Or how about the Protectorate of Oliver Cromwell in England where so much good was done along with so very many horrors? Christians were brutal to each other. What happened when the Protectorate was thrown out? British society became worse than before. Cromwell changed laws and ruled with an iron hand, but hearts were only hardened.

While we're heading east let's jump back in time to the Crusader Kingdom of Jerusalem. Those good Christian leaders empowered by the Church were amazingly effective in destroying the true message of Jesus in the Muslim world and making Christianity a stench to untold millions for a thousand years.

From that point it's just a short hop north to medieval Rome and Europe in the corrupt age of Papal power that led millions into spiritual darkness in the name of Christ and led to the brutal Inquisition. How many innocent people were murdered due to false accusations? How many Jews were persecuted and slaughtered making Christianity a stench among Jesus' own people?

I'm convinced that the men who hung my grandmother were devout believers in the Lord. It's just that their understanding of truth had been warped by their agenda of societal "needs." To meet those needs, they twisted the Bible to justify their actions. The syncretism of faith and political power was complete and righteous "ends" came to justify brutality.

The men who hung my grandmother were following the conservative agenda of their time and culture. They were trying to protect their society from the ravages of evil and lawlessness. They were trying to maintain the purity of Christianity. In doing so, they parted from the Christian faith.

When syncretism is complete it's a short journey from Plymouth Rock to the hanging tree, from the desire to worship freely, to the murder of a sister in Christ who wants to do the same. After all these years have we Christians changed?

Chapter Three

Pavlov's Christians

Another true story: Quite a number of years ago I was at a dinner party. The hostess had everything carefully planned so that her guests, who didn't know each other, might become acquainted. At the table I was seated next to an attractive woman whom I had just met.

The evening was going along quite well, the food was delicious and the conversation pleasant. Talk had quieted as we focused on eating when, suddenly, my dinner partner let out a horrific SHRIEK.

Jerking back, she stared at me as though I had just spit in her food. Now any male who has been married longer than 20 minutes knows that when a woman stares at you and shrieks you'd better come up with a serious apology for *something*. But for the life of me, I couldn't think of anything that I had done. Was she offended to the point of madness because I had used the wrong fork? All I could do was stare helplessly at her.

Here is what had happened. Unseen by any of us, the family's large cat had slithered under the table. Then, like the demon-possessed creature that it was, it had decided to destroy my reputation. Squatting in front of my dinner partner it had reached up and grabbed her nylon-covered thigh on both sides above the knee. When the claws dug in, she thought it was my fingers.

Let me tell you before that cat crawled out there were a few tense moments while I tried to prove that both my hands had been occupied eating and my nails were really short. Only when she saw the monster slink away was she convinced.

The truth is, pitiful creatures that we are, like Pavlov's dogs, most of our lives are spent responding thoughtlessly to psychological conditioning. The unpleasant sensation on my dinner partner's leg triggered a set of memories, which in turn, triggered an intense emotional response. If that cat had managed to escape without being seen I would have been the main course for dinner.

We don't like to think about psychological conditioning. We like to believe that all of our choices are made deliberately with the full weight of logic and experience behind them. Unfortunately, it just isn't so. Within each of us resides a universe of knee-jerk emotional responses conditioned by the general nastiness of human life. Even more troubling is the reality that we swim in a sea of carefully planned media conditioning designed to influence us. How powerful is that influence?

I'm an old guy who was a child in the 1950's. When I was a kid I loathed cottage cheese. But every day at lunch I would watch a TV show hosted by a Chicago celebrity who called himself Uncle Johnny Coons. Every single day Uncle Johnny would open up a carton of his sponsor's cottage cheese and start shoveling it into his mouth as though it were ice cream. Every day I watched him groan with pleasure at the first bite.

Well, I wanted to groan with pleasure, so after watching him do this for a year I started eating the stuff. Do you know I actually began liking it? I mean, it took awhile. The first few bites made me gag. But I was sure Uncle Johnny wouldn't steer me wrong, so I worked at it. My mother was staggered. She couldn't get anything down my throat that wasn't made of chocolate. Unfortunately, a lot of media conditioning isn't quite as harmless as getting kids to eat slimy curds.

For decades, Americans have been conditioned by what might be called the "Politics of Panic." I remember crawling under my desk at school during the nuclear attack drills of the 1950's. I was a big kid and I knew that any part of me not protected by that desk would be burned to ashes.

It was a fearful choice for a child. What was I going to lose this time, my legs or my butt? Usually, I opted for the legs. I mean, you can live without legs. But I'd never seen anybody live without a butt.

It was during those drills that I lost all faith in government. I was only ten, but I could see right through this foolishness. If they really wanted to protect kids from a nuclear holocaust they would have given us bigger desks.

Just like that, a little conservative was born. If my butt was going to be saved, government wasn't going to do it for me. Also, just like that, I developed a whole set of odd little quirks and foibles. All these years later I have a tendency to believe that disaster is looming just over the horizon and I need to be near a very large desk. (That isn't to say that disaster *isn't* looming. I think it is. Well, you see what I mean?)

Wherever we are on the political spectrum, the "Politics of Panic" continue to condition us. For many years we have been groomed to respond in a particular way to a set of code words such as "abortion," "homosexual marriage," "illegal aliens," "liberal judges," "the ACLU," "assault weapons," "gun control," "global warming," etc. No matter which side of the political spectrum we are on, like Pavlov's dogs, when such code words are "rung" we "salivate" with fear, fury and frustration.

For evangelical Christians, the blistering blather of talk radio and the so-called 24-hour "news" cycle urges us to remain at a high level of reactionary fervor. Here is an unpleasant truth: For the political and media elites, negative emotion is a positive response.

I spent too many years in Hollywood as a writer and executive producer in television not to understand the importance of "locking in" your audience. First, you draw them in with fiery "teasers," then you pull every trick in the book to keep them from changing the channel.

Fearful, furious and frustrated people don't change channels. They use the commercial breaks to rant about what they've just heard. I know, because it's one of my favorite pastimes. The bell rings and I start a good, long, salivating rant that carries me right on through to the next program segment.

Because these negative emotions are contagious, they build big audiences and big audiences mean big money for big corporations. Political parties love fear, fury and frustration because they energize constituencies to give money and get out the vote. With the rise of "social" media we don't even need big corporations and political parties to manipulate us into fear, fury and frustration. We can do it to each other.

Have you noticed that fear, fury and frustration seem to be essential for both liberal and conservative existence? Have you ever met a dedicated liberal or conservative who appeared to be joyful and filled with peace? I haven't.

In fact, if you are joyful and filled with peace, good conservatives and liberals are apt to think that you are a mindless airhead hopelessly out of touch with the desperate issues of life. Yet, according to my reading of the Bible, in spite of all the darkness around us, joy and peace are to be the attributes of a true follower of Jesus in this world.

Here is what I know: I can't be fearful, furious and frustrated and have the peace of Jesus. I can't be fearful, furious and frustrated and make truly Christian decisions. Most of all, I can't be fearful, furious and frustrated and carry out the Great Commission. When I fall into this pattern of conditioning, I start to believe the lie that the crises of my world are essentially political in their origins and political in their solutions.

When I think like a conservative instead of a Christian, the Republican Party, guided by a good Tea Party political agenda, appears to be the only hope for the salvation of society. That, my friend, is heresy. We may say that's not what we believe, but our words and actions prove otherwise.

Now, I'm no scholar, but I've done quite a bit of reading and thinking about the history of Western culture and why it has been so successful in the liberation of humanity compared to other cultures of the world. The primary difference has been the Gospel (which means Good News) of Jesus Christ.

Western culture was transformed by the message of Jesus Christ proclaimed fearlessly through His Church to pagan empires and barbarian tribes. The Church failed in those periods when it stopped being a servant and tried to be the ruler. It failed when it cast off the "cross of culture" and tried to wear "culture's crown." During those periods when it functioned in the full power of missionary servanthood, the Church proved itself to be the *only* agent for long-term liberating change in the world.

To most liberals and many conservatives, such a statement sounds like fundamentalist claptrap. But there is a huge weight of evidence that proves it to be true. What generated the greatest moral transformation in the history both of this country and of England? A period in the early 1700's called the Great Awakening. Under the powerful Gospel preaching of men like Whitefield and Wesley many thousands heard the message of salvation in Jesus Christ and their lives were transformed. That is what changed our society at its foundation. That is what created the true seedbed of freedom. Without it, whatever happened in Philadelphia in 1776 would not have taken hold.

Tragically, most 21st century evangelical Christians, victims as they are of secularist historical revisionism, know little about that period of our history. And if they learned of it, they wouldn't believe that it relates to today. Certainly, President George W. Bush understood little about the need for such a seedbed for freedom. Consequently, he and his generals stumbled naively into Iraq believing that "people just want to be free" and democratic freedom can be planted anywhere.

For several decades, most Christians of my persuasion have believed that if we want to save American culture we must vote Republican, sign petitions, go to Tea Party rallies, slap on bumper stickers and give money to conservative causes. It's our only hope. We must bend that stubborn old Republican Party, so full of RINOs, to our will. When they are properly bent, we will reward them with our votes.

Here is the unfortunate truth: *We did it and we failed.*

When it was in power, we expected the Republican Party to "Reshape America" according to our image. To get our votes, they promised over and over to take our concerns seriously on a whole litany of "moral issues" such as ending abortion on demand, keeping homosexual marriage illegal, dealing with illegal aliens, reestablishing God and prayer in schools, etc.

It was all a great quid pro quo. While the Party did its part, we would do ours. To the Party, in addition to getting out the vote, the job of the Church was to become an outlet for "Compassionate Conservatism," doing what they think we do best – hugging people, helping the down-and-out get a leg up in the world and building good, strong families with solid "traditional values." Republicans think evangelical Christians are just Mormons who don't send their kids out on bicycles in white shirts and ties.

The promise was that if all of us worked together under the "big tent" of the GOP, our culture would be renewed. Was the promise true or was it nothing more than a deadly distraction that took our eyes off the real work of transformation?

Chapter Four

The Old Whore
Bangs on the Door

Back in 2005 I wrote this on my blog: I appreciate the fact that the Republican Party values the Church as opposed to many Democrats who would prefer that churches be like abortions – legal, safe, and rare. But I fear the loving embrace of the Republican Party, because I don't believe for a moment that most Republican leaders want the Church to be who Jesus wants us to be.

Truthfully, neither party yearns to face large numbers of independent, clear-thinking Christians. Both the left and the right would like to enlist the support of a safely neutered Church easily turned by the bit and bridle of manipulated emotions.

But Christianity that is real can't be controlled by any force within this world. It was born in blood and agony in the screaming nightmare of a Roman execution and the blazing Light from an empty tomb. It was born from a shattering Love that knows no equal, a Love that is an all-consuming Fire, untamable in its Majesty, erupting with Power, transforming the catastrophe of death into the Joy of an Eternal Song.

That's the Christianity that the Republican Party and many evangelical leaders have tried to syncretize (read that "tame down and integrate") with a pallid, conservative, political agenda in order to "transform" society. If our Christianity is real, that will be like trying to syncretize a volcano with a sputtering methane garbage dump vent. But, maybe it isn't real. Maybe for most of us, our form of "Christianity" syncretizes quite well.

Is it my imagination or do I see the results of easy syncretism all around us? When our faith is syncretized with a political agenda we fall quickly into the Second Temptation offered by the Curse of Conservatism: We give up personal responsibility to think and act "Christianly" with regard to the crises of our world.

Instead, we let others think for us and tell us how to respond. On every practical level, we stop believing that any answers exist other than those offered by the syncretized agenda. When those fail, we wring our hands with even more fear, fury and frustration. Eventually, when the whole agenda comes crashing down (as most assuredly it will), we retreat into fully neutered isolation.

I wrote those words in 2005. Now in 2013 it's clear that the Grand Syncretized Agenda has come crashing down. When it was in power, the Republican Party proved itself to be very much like its hated opponents. Now in 2013, the GOP is in disarray, at war within itself.

And what is the party's attitude toward the evangelical Church? From viewing her as a lovely nubile young woman to be courted, many of the Republican elite see the Church as a worn-out whore. They've slept with her, used her, and didn't get the pleasure they wanted. So now they're searching for a more desirable wench. (How about the Hispanic community? How about gays?) Like an old mistress who has been discarded, the Church is shrieking and pounding on the bedroom door. Well, we deserve what has happened to us. Do you think I am over-dramatizing the situation?

In September of 2012 there took place an ultimate aberration, a startlingly clear image of that raging old evangelical whore fighting to matter to the lovers who had rejected her. It happened when the largest "evangelical Christian" university in the world – Liberty University of Lynchburg, VA – invited Donald Trump, a false prophet of egomania, wealth and narcissism if ever there was one, to address their fall convocation. He gave them the message from the god he serves, Mammon. It was a call to pride and vengeance and it was received with joy. If ever there was a moment when the Curse of Conservatism, the Curse of Syncretism, the whoredom of American evangelicalism was displayed for the entire world to see, it was that day.

Are you sick of it yet? Is your stomach churning? Do you feel a cold horror deep inside? If you don't, I have nothing more to say to you. But if you're sick of the evangelical Christianity in America that worships the false god of money, fame and power, if you're tired of abdicating personal responsibility for cultural transformation to a political machine, then stay with me.

I know this, if I'm ever going to break free from my cultural conditioning, from my enslavement to the sin-wreaked groping blindness that pervades the evangelical Church in America, I need to figure out what it means to think and act "Christianly" in my world.

Thank God we are not left to dither about this. Micah 6:8 says it all: "He has showed you, O man, what is good. And, what does the Lord require of you? To act justly and to love mercy and to walk humbly with your God."

Now, that is a truly radical agenda. How at odds is it with the political agendas that are being offered to us? Would Donald Trump find it to his liking? I think it would make him throw up. If Republicans and Democrats were rewriting the Bible here's the way that verse would read: "We have shown you, oh person, what is good. And what does the Party require of you? To vote selfishly and to love power and to walk fearfully under our control."

But how can we "act justly" and "love mercy" with regard to the crises of our time? Isn't the first step to be fearlessly and openly honest? Doesn't walking humbly with God mean believing that Jesus can and will share His radical thoughts with us as we face the issues of life?

Over many years, I've discovered that Jesus' thoughts are never comfortable. Very often, I don't like them. They force me to examine my decisions in a way that is not natural to my selfish, fearful and furious inclinations. Always He demands that radical transformation begin in the hearts of those who claim to follow Him. I'd like to try to apply that principle to a burning issue of our day...homosexual marriage.

Chapter Five

Let's All Destroy
Marriage Together

All the political pundits on both the left and the right seem to agree that in November of 2004 George W. Bush was elected in large part because evangelical Christians were energized to vote by the challenge of homosexual marriage. That was the issue that drove us to the polls. The Defense of Marriage Act signed by President Bill Clinton in 1996 wasn't enough. Much more had to be done.

In a number of states the issue of homosexual marriage was a ballot initiative and across the country it was a burning topic in the minds of everyone. For months, the subject was roasted in the conservative media. Over and over, it was pounded into us that if we lost on that issue, the family would be destroyed and our country would go down with it.

When that November came, we evangelicals rose up in righteous indignation. The line was drawn in the sand. We had to save marriage. George W. Bush was to be our standard-bearer. He would lead the charge against the tide of the liberal judiciary. He would stop the activist judges who are destroying the moral fabric of America. We were assured that even if the ballot initiatives failed in the courts, President Bush would push through a constitutional amendment that would make marriage between one man and one woman forever.

Let's try for some fearless honesty? On the face of it, every one of those ballot initiatives and the idea of a constitutional amendment are a sham. Having a million homosexuals get "married" means nothing as far truly "saving marriage and the family" are concerned.

If only evangelical Christians really did want to save marriage and the family. But it's clear that we don't. If you're getting furious with me right now, may I suggest that it's because of media conditioning?

Think with me for a moment. How can I say that we really don't want to save marriage? How can I say that all of those expensive initiatives were worthless? Am I in favor of homosexual marriage? Categorically, I am not. When it is instituted, and I believe absolutely that it will be instituted, it will prove to be a curse in ways that are unforeseen, a curse for homosexuals as well as for everyone else. But, let's pursue the truth wherever it leads.

What effect will the legalization of homosexual "marriage" have on the disastrous state of marriage in this country? Absolutely none. Even George W. Bush was in favor of "civil unions." What's the difference between a homosexual marriage and a civil union? After reading all the arguments, I don't see any. These are meaningless categories created by Machiavellian hacks.

The brutal truth is this: We don't want homosexuals to destroy marriage because we Christian heterosexuals want the freedom to do it ourselves. We enjoy our no consequences "serial monogamy." I would believe that all of those initiatives and a constitutional amendment might mean something if they included a single change in the current law – the end of no-fault divorce.

If we really want to save marriage shouldn't the first step be to make divorce difficult? It used to be. But decades ago we heterosexuals decided that issues of morality should not be in question when a husband and wife wanted to burn their marriage vows.

It was embarrassing and unnecessary to point a finger of guilt based on outmoded moral codes. It was embarrassing and unnecessary to let the world see the petty selfishness, ugliness and immorality that had led two people to destroy their family. After all, when a marriage ends aren't both parties equally at fault? Why should we point a judgmental finger at one as opposed to another? That's the "wisdom" that prevailed.

Now No-Fault Divorce is institutionalized and aren't we enjoying its benefits? Apparently, there has been at least one. Since it became law, spousal abuse has markedly decreased. That is a very good thing. But let's balance it against another hellish reality. During the same period youth violence has hideously increased.

When I was a kid in the 1950's, in my grade school class of about 25 there were only one or two who came from broken homes. Youth violence was virtually nonexistent. In my granddaughter's grade school class just a few years ago, with about the same number of kids, there were only one or two who DIDN'T come from broken homes.

The social experiment of the 1960's that has applied utter selfishness and narcissism to marriage and parenthood and rides on the back of easy divorce is the direct cause of the vast majority of the violence we see in our society. Children without parents, especially without fathers! Young men growing up with no fathers present in their lives!

We are generations into a fatherless society. What is the result? Many young men (and older men), who didn't have any fathers, now live with so much rage and self-loathing that they lash out in violence and murder.

We are governed by fools who refuse to see and accept root causes. And there are greater fools getting divorces every day. Our children are broken. Yet, do we want to deal with the root cause, the evil of divorce? Not if it might limit our selfishness. Consequently, our society is cursed. We have cursed ourselves. And we have only begun to see what that will mean in the future.

In the distant past, every divorce was a cautionary tale to those who were still married. Do you want to experience the opprobrium of society as you cast off your spouse? Well, there is no more opprobrium and marriage means little. Do we want to make a serious legal statement that marriage between a man and a woman is vital to society? End No-Fault Divorce.

But I assure you, it will be a cold day in hell before a good conservative politician proposes that. After all, many of them, like the Honorable Mr. Newt Gingrich, have already made use of No-Fault Divorce to toss away multiple spouses. In his case, this was followed by a long period of wallowing public repentance during his Presidential bid. And these are the people we believe will lead us in "Reshaping America."

So in 2004 we evangelical Christians stomped to the polls to "defend" marriage. With desperate prayers on our lips, we watched the tabulation of election results hoping against hope that our politicians would be elected so that marriage would be saved.

Why did we bother when we aren't saving it in our own churches? Oh yes, we sob about divorce; we counsel and cry and hug. And what good has it done? The divorce rate among evangelical Christians remains hellishly high.

Do we really want to defend marriage? If the answer is "yes," may I suggest that the first step is a period of agonizing repentance for our own sloth and hypocrisy? And then before we try to set up rules to save marriage in society, it might be a good idea to set up a few to save it in our own congregations. Here are four proposals to make a start:

1. To be a member of an evangelical church you must agree never to use pornography. Do we not all understand that pornography is a key factor in the destruction of marriage? According to a 2003 Focus on the Family survey, 47% of Christian families said pornography is a problem in their home. Do you think the situation has improved in the past ten years? Over half of evangelical pastors admit viewing pornography last year. (http://www.archomaha.org/pastoral/se/pdf/PornStats.pdf) Forget about saving marriage in society until we deal with such root evil among ourselves.

Here's an interesting question: How many pastoral search committees have ever asked a prospective candidate to bring his personal computer in for examination by an expert who would expose all the deleted files? How many members of a pastoral search committee or elder board would be willing to undergo that kind of scrutiny themselves?

Do you want to be assured of the spiritual maturity of your leadership? Then try it in your church. The measure of the negative response will be a measure of your problem. Do you think such a requirement is insulting and unnecessary? If you do, either you're a porn addict yourself or you are abysmally naive. The fact that we need to start taking such measures speaks to the depth of our crisis.

2. The only marriages performed in evangelical churches shall be "covenant marriages." If you don't know what that is, do a web search. Simply stated, a covenant marriage is a contract that is much more difficult to dissolve than a typical set of marriage vows. The parties who agree to it know what they are doing and their commitment to making their marriage work is much deeper.

3. No marriage shall be performed for any couple who is living together until they have lived apart for at least nine months (after all, like a baby, something new is being born), abstaining from sexual relations and undergoing in-depth *discipleship* counseling. The statistics are clear. People who live together before marriage have a much higher divorce rate and I have a sneaking suspicion that most of them are spiritual illiterates.

   (Of course, today many young people live together and don't get married at all, so divorce rates don't count.) If people knew what it really meant to follow Jesus and accepted the life-long challenge of discipleship, would it make a difference in their marriages? I'm sure it would. So why do we shut our eyes to this destructive situation? Why don't we do something about it?

4. For the party in a divorce who bears primary responsibility for the dissolution, we should make his or her choice mean something more than a big hug of welcome into the singles fellowship group. We should reinstitute church discipline for immorality. We should stop being afraid to be called "judgmental." We should start judging righteously in dealing with sin. And, yes, we may be sued.

5. If a person is found to be responsible for the dissolution of a marriage and that individual is a pastor, elder or deacon, he or she should not be able to hold such a position of leadership again. There are many other places of service within the Body of Christ after true repentance. Restoration should not mean that we put them back into the same positions.

I have heard the argument that if they aren't reinstated the Church will lose their spiritual gifts. That's absurd. Can God not raise up others with such gifts? I have heard the argument that they must be reinstated because it's the only way to show love and forgiveness. That, also, is absurd. In such situations, what we call exercising love and forgiveness, which are the vital hallmarks of Christianity, become a means of "cheap grace." Certainly, it has cheapened the vows of marriage. We mirror our leaders and their actions.

All of that said, those who are the innocent parties in a divorce should not be banned from Church leadership. Why impose punishment that they do not deserve when they are suffering already? Not in any way, should they be viewed as second-class citizens within the Body of Christ. If a person was robbed or raped would we exclude them from full participation? Of course not. Neither should it happen here.

If every evangelical church in the United States took such stands it would mean a true "defense of marriage." From a foundation of righteousness we might begin to regain our voice in calling society to repentance, which is the only hope for lasting cultural transformation.

Will it happen? Not as long as we condemn others before we judge ourselves. Not as long as we depend on a legislative agenda to save us from the consequences of our sins.

Forgive me for being cynical, but I'm sure none of these proposals will be implemented. We aren't quite that serious about saving marriage. So at least we should stop being hypocrites. Let's forget about defending "marriage." Let's welcome the Gay community into the civil unions that we call marriage that have replaced real marriage throughout our culture. At least we would be honest and there's something to be said for that.

But it's time to examine the Third Temptation in the Curse of Conservatism – the temptation to let politics and power strangle our witness to the world.

Chapter Six

Does Discipleship Cost Anything?

Let me introduce a friend of mine from the past. I'll call him Arny. That's not his real name. I want to protect his privacy. I met Arny in 1979 just as I was beginning my professional career in Hollywood. I was a novice writer and Arny was a pro.

A couple of years previously he had been on the writing staff of one of the most successful comedy series in the history of television, a series that today is considered a cultural classic. But that wasn't all. He had also co-created another wildly popular series that had launched the career of a major Hollywood comedy film star.

Arny's success as a comedy writer was understandable. Half the things that came out of his mouth made you laugh. My friend is a gentle, funny man. I want to tell his story because few people have heard it and it shouldn't be forgotten.

At the pinnacle of Arny's career, when he was achieving the kind of success that other writers only dream about, he discovered that it wasn't enough. There was something missing. His soul was empty. It was then that an amazing thing happened. Though Arny was Jewish, he met Jesus and discovered that He is the Messiah. In that discovery, his life was transformed.

Now it goes without saying that in those days there weren't many believers in Jesus in Hollywood and almost none at Arny's level. There are a few more today, but the ones who have come in the decades since have learned how to camouflage their faith. They've learned how to "play the game" because, unless you "play the game," there's no hope of having a long comfortable career. Well, it wasn't that Arny didn't want a long comfortable career. The problem was he just couldn't conceal his joy.

When you're a writer on the staff of a television series you spend night and day with a small group of other writers. These people become like your family.

While the series is in production you spend more time with them than you do with your real family.

During those endless writer meetings gulping down piles of sandwiches and bottomless pots of coffee, you talk about everything – problems with your kids, your marriage breaking up, politics, you name it. So it's natural if something wonderful happens to you that you would want to share it with the people who have become such close friends. And that's what Arny did. He told them about how Jesus was bringing joy into his life.

I think their first reaction must have been laughter. Arny was a funny guy and obviously, this was a joke. When they realized it wasn't a joke, they were shocked. Then came the coldness. Almost overnight, old friends weren't friends anymore.

It wasn't long before he was unemployed. With Arny's professional credentials he should have been able to land another job almost instantly. But for some reason all the doors were closed.

In Hollywood, that bastion of free speech where the First Amendment is worshipped like the Holy Grail, in Hollywood, where they still wring their hands and moan over the blacklists of the McCarthy era, in Hollywood, that center of pop culture and cutting edge technology that masks the bigotry of a 19th century village in eastern Europe, Arny found that he had some "employment problems."

It was as though his career had contracted ebola. As he watched, it began to hemorrhage. I met him when it was in the final stages of bleeding to death, but while he was still hoping for a miracle. The miracle never came.

To his eternal credit, Arny never gave up his faith. If he had, all would have been forgiven. Just a simple act of contrition, a quiet renunciation of this Jesus foolishness and his former colleagues would have welcomed him back with open arms.

After all, the good, liberal-minded folk of Hollywood are nothing if not forgiving. They understand that the best of us have nervous breakdowns, snort a little too much coke, get sued for sexual harassment, cheat on a spouse, run up a string of DUI's, embezzle a little money, in other words, go slightly insane for a season. And after we're detoxed from our insanity, whether it's booze or babes or believing in Jesus, everything can be made right again. Just look at Bob Dylan.

And I know others who have done it, others who walked away from their "Jesus addiction" and are now enjoying renewed careers. Arny refused to do that because he knew that what he had gained was worth far more than anything he could lose.

And he lost a lot.

Not only did his career bleed to death, his wife divorced him. Spouses often do that when the money stops. Sometime around 25 years ago, my friend quietly left Hollywood and moved back east. It's a hard thing to give up your dreams. It's a harder thing to lose the people you love. But I'm certain of this: The reward for Arny's faithfulness is yet to come.

How does the story of my friend relate to what I've called the Curse of Conservatism?

In 1981, the Writers Guild of America decided to strike. As a new member of that guild (all writers in Hollywood are required to be union members), I had never participated in a strike and participation was mandatory.

I'll never forget that first strike meeting. It was held at the Hollywood Palladium. Twenty-two hundred writers were gathered in the grand ballroom, almost all the writers responsible for the creation of popular culture in television and film. With me was my friend Arny.

As we sat down, I remember asking him how many people in that room might be serious Christians. He laughed and said he was pretty sure that he knew them all. Including us, maybe there were five or six.

I realized that around me in that huge room sat a microcosm of the new America. Whoever controls the creation of stories controls culture. And within my fellow writers, the new stories of America were being born.

I had grown up in Wheaton, Illinois, a small town that was a center of evangelical Christianity. But as I sat in the Hollywood Palladium, Wheaton, Illinois felt as far away as a distant star. What lay before me was the reality of a post-Christian, post-modern, neo-pagan world.

I held no illusions about that world. To varying degrees, most of the people in it were hostile to what I believed. Not that all of them hated evangelical Christians, although a significant percentage surely did. At a minimum, I knew that I was going to face distrust and potential rejection.

To be honest, I couldn't blame the people of Hollywood for their distrust. Many of them had never personally known an evangelical believer in Jesus. Their only contact with my world was flipping past tele-evangelists and getting hate mail.

With far too much historical evidence to prove them correct, they believed that anyone who called himself an evangelical Christian was probably a fool and a bigot. Not wanting to be either, I faced a crisis.

There at the beginning of my career how was I to live? What should I stand for? What risks should I take? As I considered those questions, Arny's experience loomed large before me. Did I want to relive my friend's disaster? Not if I could help it.

An immediate solution presented itself: I could split my life in half. There would be the "Christian Coleman" and the "writer/producer Coleman." In my "Christian life" with my Christian friends, I could be vocal about my faith. In my "Hollywood life" I would be silent and go into the closet for the next 20 years.

To make the closet more comfortable I could upholster it with a series of convenient lies. The first one sounded reasonable and it stroked my ego: "You're talented, but you have to earn the right to be heard and that's going to take a long time. So say nothing about what you believe. Play the game shrewdly and someday you might be successful enough that you'll have the power to speak and write whatever you want. To take the risk too soon would be foolish and self-destructive."

What did this really mean – that at some point in the distant future when I was "bulletproof" I could fearlessly emerge from my cowardice? Even at the beginning, I knew this wouldn't work. In Hollywood no one ever becomes "bulletproof." The longer you're there, the more you realize how hard it is to achieve anything and whatever you achieve you don't want to lose. To believe this lie would mean giving up the strength to speak a single courageous word ever.

If the first lie was inadequate there was a second to bolster it and this is what it whispered: "As a professional writer you're just an employee. You aren't being hired to "spread your faith." You're being hired to entertain, to capture the largest possible audience for your employers. If you accept a job, you have an obligation to fulfill the assigned responsibility and nothing more." In

Hollywood there is an ancient hallowed axiom, "If you want to send a message buy a telegram."

Well, it may be a hallowed axiom, but no one in Hollywood really believes it. Every single story has a message. Excellent writing is always passionate writing and passionate writing always comes from firmly held beliefs.

There are plenty of passionate writers in Hollywood – leftists, gays, feminists, environmentalists, Vegans, for pity's sake even PETA members. Should a Christian writer be less passionate and courageous than someone defending stray cats? To believe this lie would mean that I would become a hack and the deeper rule of Hollywood is this: "If you let us make you into a hack we will despise you. After we've used you up we'll throw you away."

To do my best work as a professional demanded a commitment to excellence and passion. I owed excellence and passion to every employer. Most of all, I owed it to Jesus Christ. And, as far as commercial appeal was concerned, the history of western literature was on my side. The most successful stories of our civilization have had Christian redemption as their theme. (Just look at Les Miserable.) The only way to fulfill every contractual obligation was to write what I knew. Though it could express itself in many forms, what I knew was the redemption from sin found in Jesus.

Unfortunately, there was yet a third lie offering a reason to bifurcate my world. And this one sounded downright pious. "If you just play the game and keep silent you can be well paid and enjoy the consolation that whatever situation you're in would be much worse if you weren't there. As a Christian, even if you're silent, just your presence can restrain evil and keep things from being as bad as they would have been otherwise."

This would allow me to look at my hackhood as a kind of cross to bear. The end would justify the means. My life could become a perfect storm of comfort and self-pity. While I enjoyed the financial fruits of my labors, I could feel like a martyr doing the best that I could.

The logical fallacy was excruciatingly clear. If I believed this lie it would allow me to do anything from working in hardcore porn to being a guard in a Nazi concentration camp. All that was necessary to justify my involvement would be a few piddling acts of goodness. Holding back five drops of evil would allow me to swim in any rancid river that presented itself for my financial enrichment.

The best non-Christian writers would never play such shameful mind games. They would have too much self-respect. Their philosophy would be, "If you choose to swim in a sewer, swim hard and do your best to enjoy it. Don't lie to yourself about why you're there. You're there to make money. So suck it up."

Should a Christian be less honest about his motives? Money, security, and success couldn't be my ultimate goals or I would betray everything I believed about the call of God. And I felt called by Him to Hollywood.

The choice was clear. I couldn't divide my world. Like Arny, I had experienced a new life in Jesus. My whole life is based on one reality. Repentance leading to redemption through the forgiveness of Jesus is the only path to lasting joy.

That would be the theme that would guide the struggle of my career. It would mean walking for years on the brink of disaster, hoping for acceptance, ready for rejection, constantly praying for the strength, grace and mercy of God.

Having made my decision I didn't want to be stupid. I knew that I had to pick my battles wisely. In the early 1980's evangelical Christianity was deep into its decades long entanglement with Republican politics. The "Moral Majority" was on the rise. More and more people were equating being a Christian with being a Republican. Evangelical Christians were flexing their muscles. They liked the feeling of political and cultural power.

As for me, I had to be able to have quiet discussions with friends in my industry about Jesus apart from politics. I wanted people to see Him in my life and writing, not the shadow of Ronald Reagan. I hadn't come to Hollywood to spread the "Republican Faith." No Republican had died on a cross for me. To be an effective Christian in a hostile world means refusing to be distracted into conflicts that are not worth fighting.

My challenge as a Christian was to be cautious in choosing a battle, but when I entered one, to fight it fearlessly. As a writer of drama I would be dealing with moral issues. I determined that my task was to think "Christianly," not to fall automatically into the lock-step opinions of either the left or the right.

But there was an even more vital task. The people around me were far more important than any creative work that I would ever do. My responsibility was to them. Being a Christian in a hostile world means being a loyal friend to those who do not agree with me, defending and caring for them the way Jesus would and speaking about Him whenever a door opens. It means using whatever strength you have to shield those who are under attack, even if it means being attacked yourself. In Hollywood, people often suffer viciously unjust and unreasonable attacks. When that happens to you as a Christian, you must forgive. Defending others often means that you can't defend yourself.

Over the years I did a lot of stumbling and a lot of failing. But now at the end of my career, I can tell you that the choice I made was right, the purpose held.

Chapter Seven

Let's All Picket the Studio

What is a "witness?" The simplest definition is that a witness is someone who tells what he knows. The whole life of a Christian should do that. In word and deed, such a life should speak the truth of God's love to a brokenhearted and dying world.

The most awful temptation in the Curse of Conservatism is to let politics usurp and destroy our witness. So often the fire of political rage burns friendships to ashes and it is within friendships that brokenhearted people meet Jesus.

The role of the Church is to carry the cross of culture, not to wear culture's crown. In choosing to syncretize our faith with political power, we fell into a trap of hell. For 40 years the true message of Jesus has been corrupted in the minds of millions who do not know Him. There could be no greater tragedy.

One of the most illuminating moments of my career occurred in the late 1980's. I was a writer/producer at Universal Studios working on the staff of the CBS television series, The Equalizer. One day, another writer/producer on the show and I decided to go to lunch. My friend is not a Christian. As we drove out the front gate of the studio we were surrounded by a huge crowd waving placards.

It so happens that we had decided to go to lunch at the same moment when 25,000 of my fellow believers, called to action by "Christian" radio, had arrived to protest the release of a film called "The Last Temptation of Christ." As far as that crowd was concerned, we were coming from the wrong direction. We were the enemy.

Placards bearing John 3:16 and a variety of Christian slogans were thrust at my windshield. As we drove through the singing, chanting mass, my friend turned to me and said, "Coleman, if I didn't know you, I would hate these people."

Whenever the Church tries to use the power of the world to transform society, we get exactly the opposite of what we desire. What did that display of selfishness and pseudo-power outside the studio gain for the Church? The film, which was a pathetic piece of feces, got a worldwide audience that it never would have gained without such notoriety.

Hollywood hardened itself even more to the demands of Christians. Worst of all, good people like my friend were confirmed in their belief that the only thing evangelical Christians cared about was taking away their freedom.

How had this tragedy at Universal occurred? Some of the "power players" of the evangelical world had entered the battle against that pitiful film. Bill Bright of Campus Crusade offered 10 million dollars to buy the print so it wouldn't be released. In so doing, he utterly insulted the filmmakers and studio, essentially calling them whores who cared only about money.

The insane thing was that, during that very time his organization, Campus Crusade, had an excellent ministry within Hollywood. Among its leaders were dedicated Christians who would have steered him away from such arrogant stupidity. He never called one of them. Such is the idiocy of syncretized power. For me, it was as though a horrible loop had closed. The Bill Bright of the Christian Freedom Foundation/Moral Majority conspiracy was still a thorn in my flesh, because many people at Universal knew that I was a Christian and I had to answer for him.

But he wasn't the only purveyor of arrogant stupidity. There were many other evangelical leaders who joined to bring about that debacle. James Dobson and

Focus on the Family got their fingers into that evil pie. They had transformed from a wonderful family counseling ministry into a national political pressure group. The Last Temptation was their temptation to flex some muscle.

How sad it was. I was at Universal. I understood the studio. I understood Hollywood. During the crisis, I called Dobson's organization and talked to one of his senior vice presidents. I pleaded with him that this wasn't the way to confront Hollywood. Hollywood needed to be a mission field, not a battlefield. What I confronted was mind-bending arrogance. For thirty minutes their vice president insisted on believing that I had called representing the studio to begin some kind of negotiation.

When, finally, I was able to convince him that I was just a Christian brother with special knowledge because of my position (I was the first evangelical Christian in the history of television to become the Showrunner of a successful hard-edged prime-time dramatic network series), he had no interest in talking with me at all. These men had been corrupted. They had become drunk with pseudo-power. Predictably, their failure was total.

As much as you may hate the idea, Hollywood is a microcosm of the world. After having spent many years there I can tell you that, just like the rest of the world, it is a frightened, brokenhearted place. Another writer/producer friend of mine (also not a Christian) once said to me, "Coleman, the only reason any of us come to Hollywood is to be loved."

For everyone in my industry, that desire for love leads to pain because Hollywood is a viciously abusive mother. The wonderful people of Hollywood need the love and forgiveness of Jesus, the King. The task of the Church is to live and speak the Love of God in every corner of our world and anything that stands in the way of that message is a curse.

How will we know if the Church is fulfilling her assigned task? It will be known for its peacemaking, not for its belligerence. Somehow, in the minds of many, the idea of "peacemaking" has become synonymous with mediocrity and weakness. It has come to mean lukewarm moderation, at best the expression of a neutered faith.

For many evangelical Christians, peacemaking means deal-making, a cowardly, brokered existence that does nothing more than put off the pain. But that isn't what Christian peacemaking is about at all.

Jesus bought our peace by dying on the Cross. Following in His footsteps, the true peacemaking Church lives nailed to the cross of culture, carrying within itself the agony of a fallen world, constantly dying so that lost people might know Jesus and live.

Christian peacemaking is dangerous because it is fearless and owes allegiance to no one but God. Christian peacemaking means walking in the no-man's land between the battle lines. In a world filled with hate, the peacemaking Church stands for the true justice and mercy of God's love. It thinks and acts under the power of the Holy Spirit, not under the power of a political agenda. Such a Church will make bitter enemies on every side. Have we forgotten that in Jesus' day both the liberals (the Sadducees) and the conservatives (the Pharisees) wanted to kill Him? Did He not say that the servant is no better than his master?

Here is the cold truth: We vest our hopes in a political agenda because we don't want the risk and discomfort that following Jesus will bring. We don't follow in His footsteps because we don't like the places where He insists on walking. We have vested our citizenship in an America that is gone and will never return, rather than in the priceless and eternal Kingdom of Heaven.

We want political change because we want to be left alone to live our lives in comfort without the incursion of any post-Christian, post-modern, neo-pagan nastiness. We like our churches big so our commitment can be small. We prefer boycotts, petitions and protests over prayer. We fight to save the lives of unborn babies, but care little if those babies grow up to die bloody deaths on our streets. (Unless, of course, it happens on our street.)

We hate Hollywood, but worship celebrities. We protest that there are not enough family films, while we watch pornography. We want our borders closed to everything but cheap products. We want to save marriage while we divorce our wives and husbands. What we want is the fuzzy warmth of a bloodless "faith" that costs nothing more than the gasoline it takes to drive to a mega-church with a Starbucks in the lobby.

Back in 2005 when I first wrote this essay, I included these words: In the near future evangelicals will feel betrayed by "their" party. The hints of that betrayal have already begun. Like political bosses, the reaction of some evangelical leaders has been to rage and threaten retribution. Those threats will spiral as the realization of failure continues to grow.

There will come a time when evangelical Christians realize that they have no party. The Big Tent has vanished. The circus has moved on without them and their dog and pony show is no longer wanted. At that point, there will be a lot of talk about "disenfranchisement." Some may try to start a new party, but that too will fail.

When all of this happens, in our ears should echo the words of the prophet Jeremiah, "Cursed is the one who trusts in man, who depends on flesh for his strength and whose heart turns away from the Lord."

Chapter Eight

Mission Field or Battlefield?

The Age of The Great Disillusionment is upon us. When, finally, we realize that America is never going to be reshaped in our image, that our dreams of the past will never be fulfilled, we will face a choice. How will we live in an increasingly hostile, pagan nation? Will we go into the closet, licking our wounds, trying to hide from reality? Or will we enter a new phase of wonderful, but dangerous, engagement?

Will we start looking at all of America as a mission field or insist that it is a cultural battlefield? Will we forgive our enemies or do what we can to take vengeance on them? Will we be willing to pay the price of a costly faith or enlist in the armies of anger? Will we be filled and guided by the Spirit of Jesus or the spirit of Donald Trump?

More than ever, I believe that the same God who loved this brokenhearted world so much that He sent His Son to die, loves the individual people of America. The question is, do we? It's easy to grow misty-eyed about the mythology of America and talk about "loving our country," while we despise millions of her citizens. It's easy to allow a nostalgic patriotism carry us into the Curse of Conservatism.

A century ago, Oswald Chambers wrote these words about prayer: "Are we living in such a vital relationship to our fellow men that we do the work of intercession as the Spirit-taught children of God? Begin with the circumstances we are in – our homes, our business, our country, the present crisis as it touches us and others – are these things crushing us? Are they badgering us out of the Presence of God and leaving us no time for worship? Then let us call a halt and get into such living relationship with God that our relationship to others is maintained on the line of intercession whereby God works His marvels."

Our syncretized "Christianity," with all of its fear, fury and frustration, makes us deaf to His Voice. Because we no longer hear Him, we lose the power to be intercessors. Instead of praying for our lost and sinful nation, we rail about politics and morality. We rage at those who disagree with us, blaming them for the destruction that is everywhere. Because citizenship in this world is our first allegiance, our faith is sidetracked and God's Power is gone, while we continue to imagine that it is there.

You may hate what I'm going to say in conclusion, but here is what I believe: Before the return of Jesus, our King, to this earth, every system of human government will have been tried and all will have failed – even the best system in history, our own here in the United States.

I love this country. It was the greatest privilege to have been born and lived here. Proudly, I have worn America's military uniform. My family has experienced the blessing of God in this land. But I believe that the wonderful adventure that was America is coming to an end, destroyed by selfishness, lust, greed, idolatry and violence – especially murderous violence to the "least of these," tiny children in the womb. We have exported our evils to the whole world. Because of this, we have been given over to violence and there is no turning back.

The seedbed of freedom that was necessary for America to spring into existence and live, is gone forever. The ground has turned to blood-drenched stone. That seedbed of freedom will not appear again until the Kingdom comes.

But I have wonderful news. The Kingdom of Heaven *is* coming. It draws closer every day and the gates are open to all who love Jesus and call Him Lord. Until it arrives (and no matter what may happen in the meantime), as citizens of that Kingdom, we Christians must be involved with passion and purity in every legitimate area of human society and culture, standing against evil and presenting the truth in word and deed, no matter the cost. But this must be done as missionaries to a brokenhearted pagan land, not "culture warriors" trying to restore the "traditional values" of 1955.

Like the early church in ancient Rome, we must defend and care for the weak and helpless. We must fight for justice for the downtrodden. We must take the message of God's love and salvation everywhere (yes, even to illegal aliens and Hollywood).

We must tell stories about how wonderful Jesus really is. We must prove that those stories are true by our lives. We must fight for the freedom to speak about Him. As long as that freedom exists, we *must* speak. When it doesn't exist, *still* we must speak. We must use these final years to the Glory of God.

What is the alternative? To continue as we are, worshipping the pagan god of Donald Trump and Ayn Rand and calling ourselves Christians, though the word has lost all meaning. The brutal truth is that, as slaves to the Curse of Conservatism, within us there will be no Power of God that can bring real, individual transformation. Consequently, in all the sorrow that is around us, and the greater sorrows that are going to come, we will have nothing to offer a dying world.

As I look back on the years I spent in Hollywood, I'm filled with gratitude. I'm glad I made the choices that I did, but they led where I knew they would. Like my friend, Arny, my time finally came. Like him, I discovered that a career is a tiny price to pay for the joy of serving a King who died for me.

As history moves toward its conclusion, how will you spend the rest of your life? Will you spend it fighting for a past that is gone? If that is what you choose, the Powers of Darkness will be well-pleased.

Coleman Luck is a Hollywood writer and executive producer known for such TV series as "The Equalizer" and "Gabriel's Fire." He is a mentalist and a member of the Academy of Magical Arts at The Magic Castle in Hollywood. His first novel, <u>Angel Fall</u>, was published in 2009 by Zondervan, a subsidiary of Harper/Collins. His second novel, <u>The Mentalist Prophecies - Book One – Dagon's Illusion,</u> was published in 2013. He is the author of <u>Proof of Heaven? A Mental Illusionist Examines the Afterlife Experience of Eben Alexander M.D. from a Biblical Viewpoint</u>. Coleman studied the Bible at the Moody Bible Institute, received his undergraduate degree from Northern Illinois University (magna cum laude) and did graduate study at both the University of Southern California and Simon Greenleaf School of Law. Coleman and his wife of 46 years, Carel Gage Luck, a fine artist, live in the mountains of central California.

Visit his website: www.colemanluck.com

For love of country

Coleman Luck – 1968
First Lieutenant - Infantry
United States Army
Mobile Riverine Force
Mekong Delta - South Vietnam

Bronze Star – Valor
Bronze Star – Meritorious Service
3 Army Commendation Medals – Valor
The Air Medal – for combat assaults by helicopter
The Combat Infantryman's Badge

Made in the USA
Monee, IL
28 January 2022